P9-DBL-567

P9-DBL-567

100 FACTS

ANCIENT ROME

100 FACTS

ANCIENT ROME

Fiona Macdonald

Consultant: Richard Tames

Sandy Creek
NEW YORK

An Imprint of Sterling Publishing
387 Park Avenue South
New York, NY 10016

SANDY CREEK and the distinctive Sandy Creek logo are registered trademarks of Barnes & Noble, Inc.

© 2001 by Miles Kelly Publishing Ltd.

This 2013 edition published by Sandy Creek.

All rights reserved. No part of this publication may be reproduced, stored in a retrieval system
or transmitted in any form or by any means (including electronic, mechanical, photocopying,
recording, or otherwise) without prior written permission from the publisher.

Publishing Director: Belinda Gallagher
Creative Director: Jo Cowan
Assistant Editor: Lucy Dowling
Volume Designer: Sally Lace
Picture Researcher: Liberty Newton
Indexer: Lynn Bresler
Production Manager: Elizabeth Collins
Reprographics: Anthony Cambray, Liberty Newton, Ian Paulyn
Archive Manager: Jennifer Hunt
Assets: Lorraine King

ISBN 978-1-4351-5083-6

ACKNOWLEDGMENTS
The publishers would like to thank the following artists
who have contributed to this book:

Brett Brecon, Chris Buzer/Studio Galante, Brian Dennington/Allied Artists,
Mike Foster/Maltings Partnership, Luigi Galante/Studio Galante,Brooks Hagan/Studio Galante,
Richard Hook/Linden Artists Ltd, Rob Jakeway, John James/Temple Rogers, Kevin Maddison,
Janos Marffy, Pete Roberts/Allied Artists, Eric Rowe/Linden Artists Ltd, Martin Sanders,
Rob Sheffield, Francesco Spadoni/Studio Galante,
Rudi Vizi, Mike White/Temple Rogers

Cartoons by Mark Davis at Mackerel

The publishers would like to thank the following sources for the use of their photographs:

Front cover: (Colosseum) Ocean/Corbis, (sky background) Samot/Shutterstock.com
Back: Tomasz Szymanski/Shutterstock.com

All other images from the Miles Kelly Archives

Every effort has been made to acknowledge the source and copyright holder of each picture.
Miles Kelly Publishing apologizes for any unintentional errors or omissions.

Made with paper from a sustainable forest

Manufactured in China
Lot #:
2 4 6 8 10 9 7 5 3 1

05/13

Contents

The center of an empire

1 Rome was a city in central Italy, and it ruled one of the world's greatest empires. An empire is made up of many different countries governed by a single ruler. Rome began around 1000BC as a village of wooden huts, but soon grew rich and powerful. It was busy, crowded, noisy, and exciting, with many beautiful buildings. By 200BC the Romans ruled most of Italy, and started to invade neighboring lands. They conquered a vast empire that stretched between what we now call Scotland and Turkey.

Capital city

2 **More than a million people lived in Rome.** By around AD300, Rome was the largest city in the world. There were citizens who could vote and serve in the army, and there were noncitizens who did not have these rights. The government was run by nobles and knights who were usually very rich. Plebeians, or ordinary people, were usually fairly poor but were citizens of Rome. Slaves were not citizens. They were not free to leave their owners and had no rights.

3 The Forum was the government district in the center of Rome. People went there to meet their friends and business colleagues, discuss politics, and to listen to famous orators who made speeches in the open air. The Forum was mainly a marketplace, surrounded by government buildings such as offices and law courts.

4 Rome was a well–protected city. It was surrounded by 30mi (50km) of strong stone walls, to keep out attackers. All visitors had to enter the city through one of its 37 gates which were guarded by soldiers and watchmen.

5 The Romans were great water engineers. They designed aqueducts, raised channels to carry water from streams in far-away hills and mountains to the city. The richest Roman homes were supplied with constant running water carried in lead pipes. Ordinary people had to drink from public fountains.

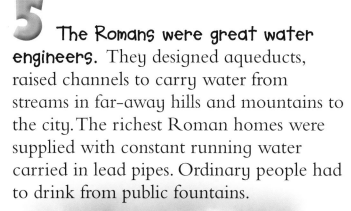

6 Rome relied on its drains. Rome was so crowded that good drains were essential. Otherwise, the citizens could have caught diseases from sewage and died. The largest sewer, called the "cloaca maxima," was so high and so wide that a horse and cart could drive through it.

I DON'T BELIEVE IT!

Roman engineers also designed public rest rooms. These were convenient, but not private. Users sat on rows of seats, side by side!

City life

7 The Romans built the world's first high-rise apartments. Most of the people who lived in Ostia, a busy port close to Rome, had jobs connected with trade, such as shipbuilders and money-changers. They lived in apartment buildings known as "insulae." A typical building was three or four stories high, with up to a hundred dirty, crowded rooms.

8 Rich Romans had more than one home. Rome was stuffy, dirty, and smelly, especially in summertime. Wealthy Roman families liked to get away from the city to cleaner, more peaceful surroundings. They purchased a house (a "villa urbana") just outside the city, or a big house surrounded by farmland (a "villa rustica") in the countryside far away from Rome.

9 Many Roman homes had a pool, but it was not used for swimming! Pools were built for decoration, in the central courtyards of large Roman homes. They were surrounded by plants and statues. Some pools had a fountain; others had mosaics—pictures made of tiny colored stones or squares of glass—covering the floor.

MAKE A PAPER MOSAIC

You will need:

large sheet of paper   scissors
pencil   glue
scraps of colored and textured paper

Draw the outlines of your design on a large sheet of paper. Plan which colors to use for different parts of the mosaic.

Cut the paper scraps into small squares, all roughly the same size. The simplest way to do this is to cut strips, then snip the strips into squares.

Stick the paper squares onto the large sheet of paper following the outlines of your design.

10 **Fortunate families had hot feet.** Homes belonging to wealthy families had underfloor central heating. Blasts of hot air, warmed by a wood-burning furnace, circulated in channels built beneath the floor. The furnace was kept burning by slaves who chopped wood and stoked the fire.

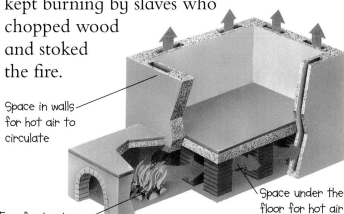

Space in walls for hot air to circulate

Fire for heating

Space under the floor for hot air

11 **Rome had a fire department.** The 7,000 firemen were all specially trained freed slaves. Ordinary families could not afford central heating, so they warmed their rooms with fires in big clay pots which often set the house alight.

Going shopping

12 Rome housed the world's first shopping mall. It was called Trajan's Market, and was built on five different levels on the slopes of the Quirinal Hill in the center of Rome. It contained more than 150 different shops, together with a large main hall.

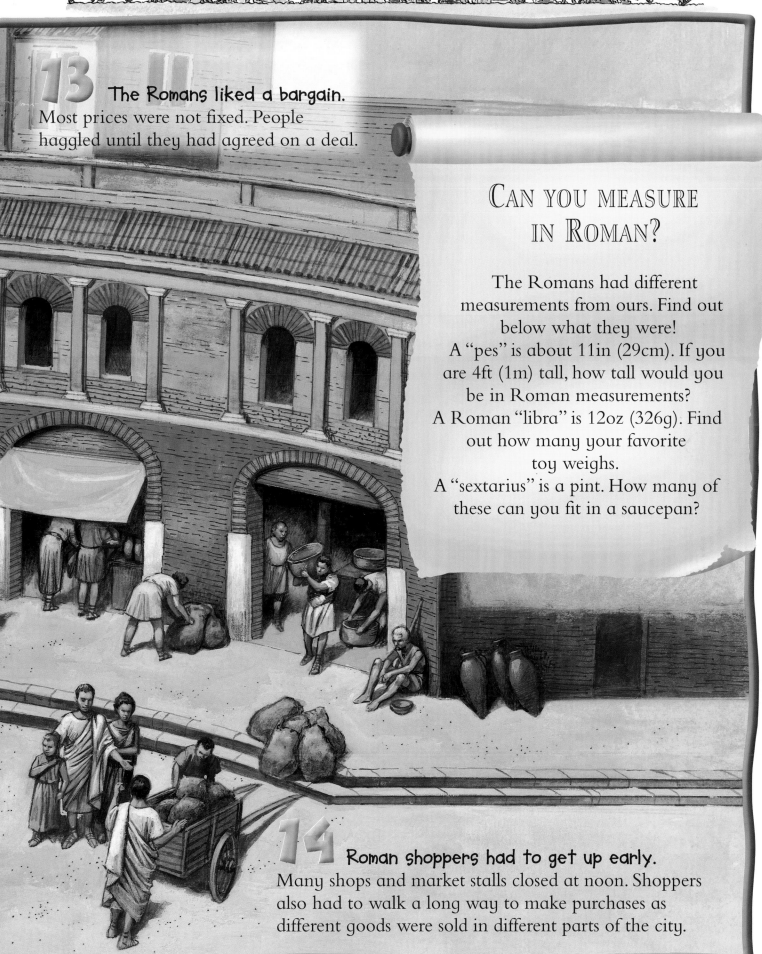

13 The Romans liked a bargain.
Most prices were not fixed. People haggled until they had agreed on a deal.

CAN YOU MEASURE IN ROMAN?

The Romans had different measurements from ours. Find out below what they were!
A "pes" is about 11in (29cm). If you are 4ft (1m) tall, how tall would you be in Roman measurements?
A Roman "libra" is 12oz (326g). Find out how many your favorite toy weighs.
A "sextarius" is a pint. How many of these can you fit in a saucepan?

14 Roman shoppers had to get up early.
Many shops and market stalls closed at noon. Shoppers also had to walk a long way to make purchases as different goods were sold in different parts of the city.

Eating and drinking

15 Most Romans ate very little during the day. They had bread and water for breakfast and a light snack of bread, cheese, or fruit around midday. They ate their main meal at about 4p.m. In rich people's homes, a meal would have three separate courses, and could last for up to three hours! Poor people ate much simpler foods, such as soups made with lentils and onions, barley porridge, peas, cabbage, and tough, cheap cuts of meat stewed in vinegar.

16

Only rich Roman people had their own kitchen. They could afford to employ a chef with slaves to help him in the kitchen. Ordinary people went to "popinae" (cheap eating houses) for their main meal, or bought ready-cooked snacks from roadside fast food stands.

17

At parties, the Romans ate lying down. Men and women lay on long couches arranged round a table. They also often wore crowns of flowers, and took off their sandals before entering the dining room. Nine was the ideal number of guests for a dinner party, but many people had more.

REAL ROMAN FOOD!

PATINA DE PIRIS (Pear Soufflé)
Ingredients:

2lb (1kg) pears (peeled and cored)	a little bit of oil
	pinch of salt
6 eggs (beaten)	$\frac{1}{2}$ tsp cumin
4 tbsp honey	ground pepper to taste

Make sure that you ask an adult to help you with this recipe.
Mash the pears together with the pepper, cumin, honey, and a bit of oil. Add the beaten eggs and put into a casserole. Cook for approximately 30 minutes in a moderate oven. Serve with a little bit of pepper sprinkled on top.

▼ Dishes served at a Roman banquet might include shellfish, roast meat, eggs, vegetables, fresh fruits, pastries, and honeyed wine. The Romans enjoyed strong-flavored, spicy food, and also sweet-sour flavors.

School days

18 Roman boys learned how to speak well. Roman schools taught three main subjects: reading, math—and public speaking! Boys needed all three skills for their future careers. There were no newspapers or television, so politicians, army leaders, and government officials all had to make speeches in public, explaining their plans and policies to Roman crowds. Boys went to school from around seven years old and left at age 16.

▼ Roman schoolboys practice reading with their slave schoolmaster.

19 Roman girls did not go to school. They mostly stayed at home, where their mothers, or women slaves, taught them how to cook, clean, weave cloth, and look after children. Girls from rich families, or families who ran a business, also learned to read, write, and keep accounts.

▼ A girl is taught to play the lyre.

20 Many of the best teachers were slaves. Schoolmasters and private tutors often came from Greece. They were purchased by wealthy people who wanted to give their sons a good education. The Greeks had a long tradition of learning, which the Romans admired.

21

The Romans wrote a lot—but not on paper. They used thin slices of wood for letters and day-to-day business. For notes Romans used flat wooden boards covered with wax, as the wax could be smoothed over and used again. For important documents that they wanted to keep, the Romans used cleaned and polished calfskin, or papyrus.

Ink pot

Pens

Stylus, to use with a wax tablet

Wax tablet

22

Romans made ink from soot. To make black ink, the Romans mixed soot from wood fires with vinegar and a sticky gum that oozed from the bark of trees. This sounds like a strange mixture, but some Roman writing has survived for almost 2,000 years.

23

Rome had many libraries. Some were public, and open to everyone, others belonged to rich families and were kept shut away in their houses. It was fashionable to sponsor writers and collect their works.

24

Many Romans read standing up—it was easier that way. It took time and patience to learn how to read from a papyrus scroll. Most were at least 30ft (9m) long. Readers held the scroll in their right hand, and a stick in their left hand. They unrolled a small section of the scroll at a time.

LEARN SOME ROMAN WORDS!

The Romans spoke a language called Latin. It forms the basis of many languages today, and below you can learn some Latin for yourself!
liber = book   epistola = letter
bibliotheca = library
vellum = calfskin
stylus = writing stick
(used with wax tablets)
librarii = slaves who work in a library
grammaticus = schoolmaster
paedagogus = private tutor

Father knows best!

25 A Roman father had the power of life and death over his family. According to Roman law, each family had to be headed by a man. He was known as the "paterfamilias" (father of a family), and was usually the oldest surviving male. The buildings of the house and its contents belonged to him, and he had the right to punish any family members who misbehaved. Even his mother and other older female relatives were expected to obey him.

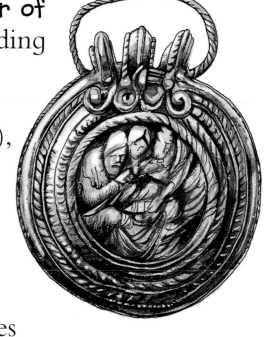

▲ The Romans gave a good luck charm, called a bulla, to their babies.

26 Roman families included more than blood relations. To the Romans, a "family" meant all the people living and working together in the same household. So families included many different slaves and servants, as well as a husband and wife and their children.

▲ This carving shows a Roman wedding, the bride and groom are in the center, with a priestess behind them.

I DON'T BELIEVE IT!

The Romans invented Valentine's Day, but called it Lupercalia. Boys picked a girl's name from a hat, and she was meant to be their girlfriend for the year!

27 Sons were valued more than daughters. The Romans preferred boys to girls. Boys would grow up to carry on the family name. They might also bring fame and honor to a family by achievements in government, politics, and war. They might marry a rich wife, which helped to make the whole family richer, or win friends among powerful people.

28 Childhood was short for a Roman girl. Roman law allowed girls to get married at 12 years old, and many had become mothers by the time they were 15. Roman girls could not choose whom to marry, especially if they came from rich or powerful families. Instead, marriages were arranged by families, to gain political power or encourage business deals. Love was not important.

29 Roman families liked to keep pets. Roman statues and paintings show many children playing with their pets. Dogs, cats, and doves were all popular. Some families also kept ornamental fish and tame deer.

Roman style

30 **Most Roman clothes were made without sewing.** Roman men and women wore loose-fitting robes, made of long strips of cloth. They were draped round the body, and held in place by pins, brooches, or belts. Most women wore several layers. These were a thin shift, a "tunica," a long, sleeveless dress called a "stola," and a thick cloak called a "palla." Men wore a knee-length tunic, a "colobium," with a semicircular cloak, a "toga," over the top.

▲ Gold brooch.

▲ Purple dye was expensive and was only worn by rich citizens. Roman senators had a purple stripe on their toga.

31 **Roman clothes were different depending on how important you were.** Ordinary men wore plain white togas, but government leaders, called senators, appeared in togas with a purple stripe around the edge. Rich men and women wore robes made of smooth, fine-quality wool and silk. Ordinary people's clothes were much rougher.

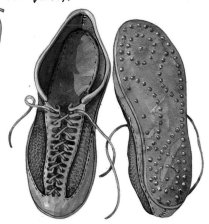

◄ This Celtic warrior from northern Europe has used dye from a plant called woad as war paint on his body.

32 Clothes told the world who you were.

People from many different cultures and races lived in lands ruled by the Romans. They wore many different styles of clothes. For example, men from Egypt wore wigs and short linen kilts. Celtic women from northern Europe wore long woolen shawls, woven in brightly colored checks. Celtic men wore trousers.

DRESS LIKE A ROMAN!

You can wear your very own toga! Ask an adult for a blanket or a sheet, then follow the instructions below!

First ask an adult to find you a blanket or sheet. White is best, like the Romans.

Drape your sheet over your left shoulder. Now pass the rest behind your back.

Pull the sheet across your front, so that you're wrapped up in it. You're almost a Roman now!

Finally, drape the last end over your right hand and there you have it, a Roman toga!

▼ These Roman sandals have metal studs in the soles to make sure that they don't wear down too quickly!

33 Roman boots were made for walking!

Roman soldiers and travelers wore lace-up boots with thick leather soles studded with iron nails. Other Roman footwear included "socci," loose-fitting slippers to wear indoors. Farmers wore shoes made of a single piece of ox-hide wrapped round the foot, called "carbatinae." There were also "crepidae," comfortable lace-up sandals with open toes.

Looking good

34 **Just like today, hairstyles changed according to fashion.** All free-born Roman women grew their hair long as short hair was a sign of slavery. In early Roman times the fashion was for plain and simple styles. Later on, most women wore their hair smoothed down and tied back tightly. Roman men usually wore short hair, and were mostly clean-shaven, except when they were old.

◄ Rich women spent a lot of time on their hair. Pins of ivory and bone were used to keep some elaborate styles in place.

35 **The Romans painted their faces.** The Romans admired pale, smooth skin. Women, and some men, used stick-on patches of cloth called "splenia" to cover spots, and wore lots of make-up. They used crushed chalk or white lead as face-powder, red ocher (crumbly earth) for blusher, plant juice for lipstick, and wood ash or powdered antimony (a silvery metal) as eyeliner.

36

Blonde hair was highly prized.
Most Romans were born with wiry dark brown hair. Some fashionable people admired delicate blonde hair, because it was unusual. Roman women used vinegar and lye (an early form of soap, made from urine and wood ash) to bleach their own hair.

37

Going to the barbers could be very painful.
In Roman times, sharp scissors and razors had not been invented. Barbers used shears to trim men's hair and beards. When a smooth, close-shaven look was in fashion barbers had to pull men's beards out by the roots, one hair at a time!

QUIZ

If you had to dress up as a Roman, what clothes would you wear? Use the information on these pages to help you draw a picture of the clothes you would need and how you might arrange your hair. Will you be a rich governor, a Celtic warrior, or a soldier?

38

Romans liked to smell sweet. They used olive oil (made from the crushed fruit of the olive tree) to cleanse and soften their skins, and perfumes to scent their bodies. Ingredients for perfume came from many different lands—flowers came from southern Europe, spices came from India and Africa, and sweet-smelling bark and resin came from Arabia.

Olive oil

Flowers to make perfume

Bark used for perfume

Star anise to make perfume

Olives

Ash to darken eyelids

Perfume bottle made of onyx, a kind of black stone

Saffron for eyeshadow

39

Roman combs were made from bone, ivory, or wood.
Like combs today, they were designed to smooth and untangle hair, and were sometimes worn as hair ornaments. But they had another, less pleasant, purpose—they were used for combing out all the little nits and lice!

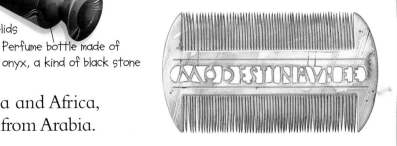

Bath time

40 The Romans went to the public baths in order to relax. These huge buildings were more than a place to get clean. They were also fitness centers and places to meet friends. Visitors could take part in sports, such as wrestling, do exercises, have a massage, or a haircut. They could buy scented oils and perfumes, read a book, eat a snack, or admire works of art in the bath's own sculpture gallery!

▼ There were public baths in most districts of Rome. They were built by Roman emperors or rich families as a gift to the citizens. The finest were the baths of Caracalla (opened around AD215), which had room for 1,600 bathers at a time.

41 Men and women could not bathe together. Women usually went to the baths in the mornings, while most men were at work. Men went to the baths in the afternoons.

The "frigidarium" had the coldest pool

The "tepidarium"' had a cool, or tepid, pool

I DON'T BELIEVE IT!

Although the Romans liked bathing, they only visited the baths once in every nine days!

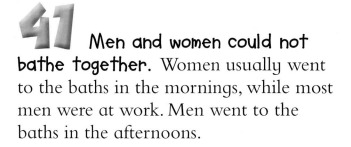

The hot room was called the "caldarium"

Fires heat the water for the hot rooms

42 Bathing wasn't simple. There were five separate stages to taking a bath Roman-style. After changing, bathers went into a very hot room, which was full of steam where they sat for a while. Then they went into a hot, dry room, where a slave removed all the sweat and dirt from their skin, using a metal scraper and olive oil. To cool off, they went for a swim in a tepid pool. Finally, they jumped into a bracing cold pool.

Having fun

43 The Romans liked music and dancing. Musicians played in the streets, or could be hired to perform at private parties. Among ordinary families, favorite instruments included pipes, flutes, cymbals, castanets, and horns. Rich, well-educated people, though, thought the noise they made was vulgar. They preferred the quieter, gentler sound of the lyre, which was played to accompany poets and singers.

▲ Roman musicians perform in the street.

Scenery could be very complicated, so it was moved around by complex machinery

Stage, or "pulpitum"

44 Romans preferred comedies to tragedies. Comic plays had happy endings, and made audiences laugh. Tragedies were more serious, and ended with misery and suffering. The Romans also liked clowns, and invented mime, a story told without words, through gestures, acrobatic movements, and dance.

45 **Plays were originally part of religious festivals.** Many famous dramas showed scenes from ancient myths and legends, and were designed to make people think about morals and politics. Later, plays were written on all sorts of topics—including politics and current affairs. Some were paid for by rich politicians, to spread their political message. They handed out free tickets to Roman citizens, hoping to win votes.

◄ All the parts in Roman plays were performed by men. For women's roles, men wore masks and dressed in female costume. Women could not be actors, except in mime.

46 **Theaters were huge well-built structures.** One of the best preserved Roman theaters is at Orange, in southern France. It has seats for almost 10,000 people. It is so cleverly designed, that the audience can hear the actors even from the back row.

47 **Roman actors all wore masks.** Masks helped the audience in big theaters see what each character was feeling. They were carved and painted in bright colors, with larger than life features and exaggerated expressions. Some masks were happy, some were frightened, some were sad.

48 **Other favorite pastimes included games of skill and chance.** Roman adults and children enjoyed dice and knucklebones, which needed nimble fingers, and checkers which relied on luck and quick thinking. They played these for fun, but adults also made bets on who would win.

I DON'T BELIEVE IT!

Roman actors were almost all men. Some were as popular as TV stars today. Women couldn't sit near the stage, in case they tried to arrange a date with one of the stars!

Let the games begin!

49 Romans admired gladiators for their strength, bravery, and skill. However, gladiators' lives were short and their deaths were horrible. They were sent to the arena to fight—and suffer—until they died.

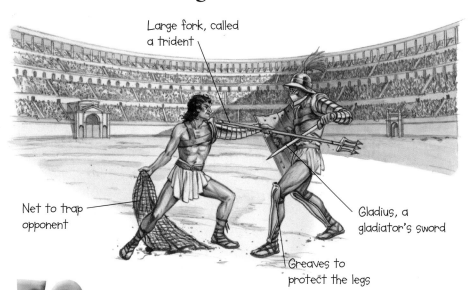

Large fork, called a trident

Net to trap opponent

Gladius, a gladiator's sword

Greaves to protect the legs

50 Most gladiators did not choose to fight. They were either prisoners-of-war or criminals who were sold to fight-trainers who organized gladiator shows. Some were specially trained, so that they would survive for longer and provide better entertainment for the watching crowds.

51 Gladiators fought wild beasts, as well as each other. Fierce wild animals were brought from distant parts of the Roman empire to be killed by gladiators in the arenas in Rome. So many lions were taken from North Africa that they became extinct there.

52 The Colosseum was an amazing building for its time. Also known as the Flavian Amphitheater, the Colosseum was a huge oval arena in the center of Rome, used for gladiator fights and mock sea battles. It opened in AD80, and could seat 50,000 people. It was built of stone, concrete, and marble and had 80 separate entrances. Outside, it was decorated with statues of famous Roman heroes.

Poles to support
a canopy

Arena

Tunnels for prisoners
and beasts

Seating for
audience

▲ The Colosseum was the largest
amphitheater in the Roman empire.

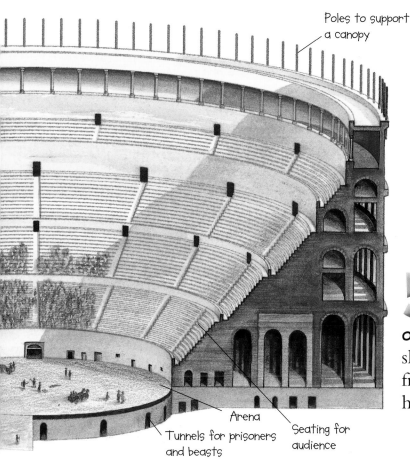

54 Chariots often collided and overturned. Each charioteer carried a sharp knife, called a "falx," to cut himself free from the wreckage. Even so, many horses and charioteers were killed.

53 Some Romans preferred a day at the races. Horses pulled fast chariots round race-tracks, called "circuses." The most famous was the Circus Maximus in Rome, which had room for 250,000 spectators. There could be up to 24 races each day. Twelve chariots took part in each race, running seven times round the oval track —a total distance of about 5mi (8km).

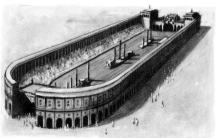

▲ The Circus Maximus.

I DON'T BELIEVE IT!

Some gladiators became so popular that people used to write graffiti about them on the walls of buildings around Rome!

55 Racing rivalries sometimes led to riots. Races were organized by four separate teams: the Reds, Blues, Greens, and Whites. Charioteers wore tunics in their teams' colors. Each team had a keen—and violent—group of fans.

Ruling Rome

56 **Rome used to be ruled by kings.** According to legend, the first king was Romulus, who came to power in 753BC.

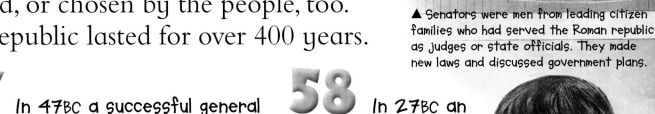

Six more kings ruled after him, but they were unjust and cruel. The last king, Tarquin the Proud, was overthrown in 509BC. After that, Rome became a republic, a state without a king. Every year the people chose two senior lawyers called consuls to head the government. Many other officials were elected, or chosen by the people, too. The republic lasted for over 400 years.

▲ Roman coin showing the emperor Constantine.

▲ Senators were men from leading citizen families who had served the Roman republic as judges or state officials. They made new laws and discussed government plans.

57 **In 47BC a successful general called Julius Caesar declared himself dictator.** This meant that he wanted to rule on his own for life. Many people feared that he was trying to end the republic, and rule like the old kings. Caesar was murdered in 44BC by a group of his political enemies. After this, there were many years of civil war.

58 **In 27BC an army general named Octavian seized power in Rome.** He declared himself "First Citizen," and said he would bring back peace and good government to Rome. He ended the civil war and introduced many strong new laws. But he also changed the Roman government for ever. He took a new name, "Augustus," and became the first emperor of Rome.

People could go to the public gallery if there was an interesting case that they wanted to see

This is a lawyer called an "advocatus." These lawyers were called in for serious cases to speak on behalf of the accused person

▲ The first rules of the Roman legal system were recorded in 450BC in a document called the Twelve Tables. The Roman system forms the basis of many legal systems today.

If the person accused of the crime refused to go to court, the prosecutor, or person accusing them, could use force to make them go. This could lead to fights

59 The Romans were proud of their laws. Everyone in Rome, from the emperor to the poorest beggar, was expected to obey the law. Roman laws were strict but fair. Everyone was considered innocent until they had been proved guilty in an open trial.

I DON'T BELIEVE IT!

Some Roman emperors were mad and dangerous. The Emperor Nero was said to have laughed and played music while watching a terrible fire that destroyed a large part of Rome.

In the army

60 Being a soldier was a good career, if you did not get killed! Roman soldiers were well paid and well cared for. The empire needed troops to defend its land against enemy attack. A man who fought in the Roman army received a thorough training in battle skills. If he showed promise, he might be promoted and receive extra pay. When he retired after 20 or 25 years' service, he was given money or land to help him start a business.

61 The Roman army contained citizens and "helpers." Roman citizens joined the regular army, which was organized into legions of around 5,000 men. Men who were not citizens could also fight for Rome. They were known as auxiliaries, or helpers, and were organized in special legions of their own.

62 Roman troops carried three main weapons. They fought with javelins, swords, and daggers. Each man had to buy his own set. He looked after them carefully—one day, his life might depend on them.

▼ Soldiers used their shields to make a protective shell. It was called a "testudo," or tortoise.

I DON'T BELIEVE IT!

Roman soldiers guarding the cold northern frontiers of Britain kept warm by wearing short woolen trousers, like underpants, beneath their tunics!

64 **The army advanced 20mi (30km) every day.** When they were hurrying to put down a rebellion, or moving from fort to fort, Roman soldiers traveled quickly, on foot. Troops marched along straight, well-made army roads. On the march, each soldier had to carry a heavy pack. It contained weapons, armor, tools for building a camp, cooking pots, dried food, and spare clothes.

63 **Soldiers needed many skills.** In enemy territory, soldiers had to find or make everything they needed to survive. When they first arrived they built camps of tents, but soon afterwards they built permanent forts defended by strong walls. Each legion contained men with a wide range of skills, such as cooks, builders, carpenters, doctors, blacksmiths, and engineers—but they all had to fight!

65 **Soldiers worshipped their own special god.** At forts and army camps, Roman soldiers built temples where they honored Mithras, their own god. They believed he protected them and gave them life after death.

▲ The Roman god Mithras wrestles with a bull.

Barracks, where soldiers sleep

Exercise yard

Gate

Protective wall

Ruled by Rome

66 More than 50 million people were ruled by Rome. Celts, Germans, Iberians, Dacians, and many other peoples lived in territory conquered by Roman armies. They spoke many different languages, and had different customs and beliefs. Roman rulers sent armies to occupy their lands, and governors to rule them. They forced conquered peoples to pay Roman taxes and obey Roman laws.

▲ A Roman tax collector assesses a farmer for taxes.

67 A few conquered kings and queens refused to accept Roman rule. For example, in AD60 Boudicca, queen of the Iceni tribe who lived in eastern England, led a rebellion against the Romans in Britain. Her army marched on the city of London and set fire to it, before being defeated by Roman soldiers. Boudicca survived the battle, but killed herself by taking poison so that she would not be captured by Roman troops.

68 Cleopatra used beauty and charm to stop the Romans invading. Cleopatra was queen of Egypt, in North Africa. Cleopatra knew that the Egyptian army would not be able to defeat Roman soldiers. Two Roman army generals, Julius Caesar and Mark Antony, fell in love with her. She stopped the Romans invading for many years, but Egypt was eventually conquered.

▼ A carving from Trajan's column of Roman legionaries boarding ships.

69 Roman conquerors built monuments to celebrate their victories. Trajan, who ruled from AD98–117, was a famous soldier who became emperor of Rome. He led Roman armies on one of their most successful conquests, in Dacia (Romania) in AD106. To record this achievement, he gave orders for a tall stone pillar (now known as Trajan's Column) to be built in the Forum in Rome. It was almost 100ft (30m) high, and was decorated with carvings of 2,500 Roman soldiers winning wars.

▲ Trajan's column.

PAINT YOURSELF LIKE A CELTIC WARRIOR!

Roman writers reported how Celtic warriors decorated their faces and bodies with patterns before going into battle. They believed that the paint was magic, and would protect them. The Celts used a deep blue dye made from a plant called woad. If you have some special face-painting make-up (make sure you ask an adult), then try making up some scary war-paint designs of your own!

▲ A carving from Trajan's column of Roman soldiers building the walls of a new fort.

The farming life

70 **Rome relied on farmers.** Most people in Roman times lived in the countryside and worked on farms. Farmers produced food for city dwellers. Without them, the citizens would not have survived. Food was grown on big estates by teams of slaves, and on small peasant farms where single families worked together.

71 **Farm produce was imported from all over the empire.** Wool and honey came from Britain, wine came from Greece, and 400,000 tons of wheat were shipped across the Mediterranean Sea from Egypt every year. It was ground into flour, which was used to make bread, the Romans' staple, or basic food.

72 **Farmers had no big machines to help them.** Heavy work was done by animals, or by human muscle-power. Plows were pulled by oxen. Ripe crops were harvested by men and women with curved knives called sickles, and loaded by hand onto farm carts. Donkeys turned mill wheels to crush olives and grind grain, and to raise drinking water from wells.

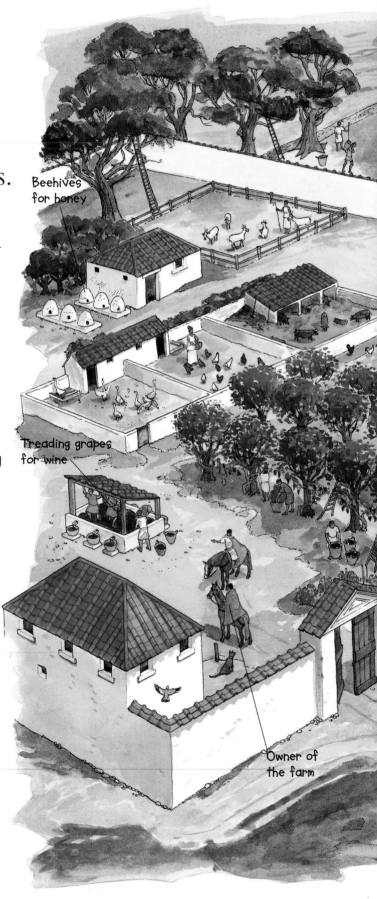

Beehives for honey

Treading grapes for wine

Owner of the farm

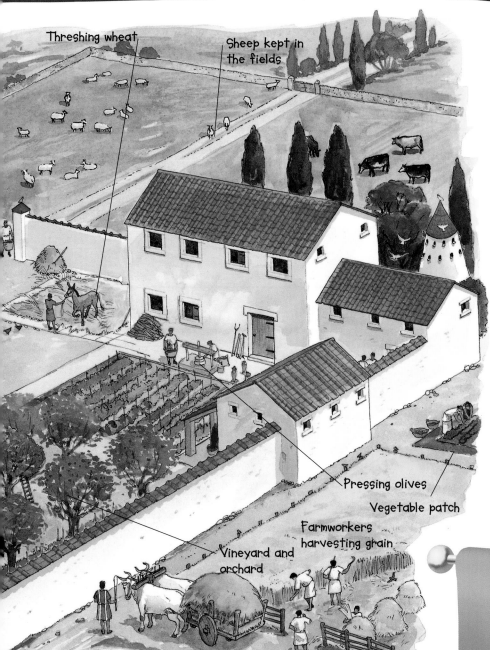

Threshing wheat

Sheep kept in the fields

Pressing olives

Vegetable patch

Farmworkers harvesting grain

Vineyard and orchard

74 The most valuable fruit was small, hard, green, and bitter! It came from olive trees. Olives could be pickled in salty water to eat with bread and cheese, or crushed to provide oil. The Romans used olive oil as a medicine, for cooking and preserving food, for cleaning and softening the skin, and even for burning in lamps.

QUIZ

Imagine that you are a Roman farmer, talking to a visitor from the city. How would you answer their questions:

What crops do you grow?
Why do you keep oxen?
Who will harvest that grain?
How do you grind grain into flour?
Why are you growing olives?

73 Roman grapes grew on trees! Vines, climbing plants that produce grapes, were planted among fruit trees in Roman orchards. They provided support for the vine stems, and welcome shade to stop the grapes getting scorched by the sun. Grapes were one of the most important crops on Roman farms. The ripe fruits were picked and dried to become raisins, or pulped and made into wine.

Work like a slave!

75 Roman people were not all equal. There were different classes within Roman society. Throughout the Roman empire, the biggest difference between people was whether they were slaves or free. Free-born men and women had rights that were guaranteed by law, for example, to find their own work, or travel from one place to another. In Rome, citizens also had the right to vote for government officials, and to receive free handouts of food. But slaves had hardly any rights at all. They belonged to their owners just like dogs or horses.

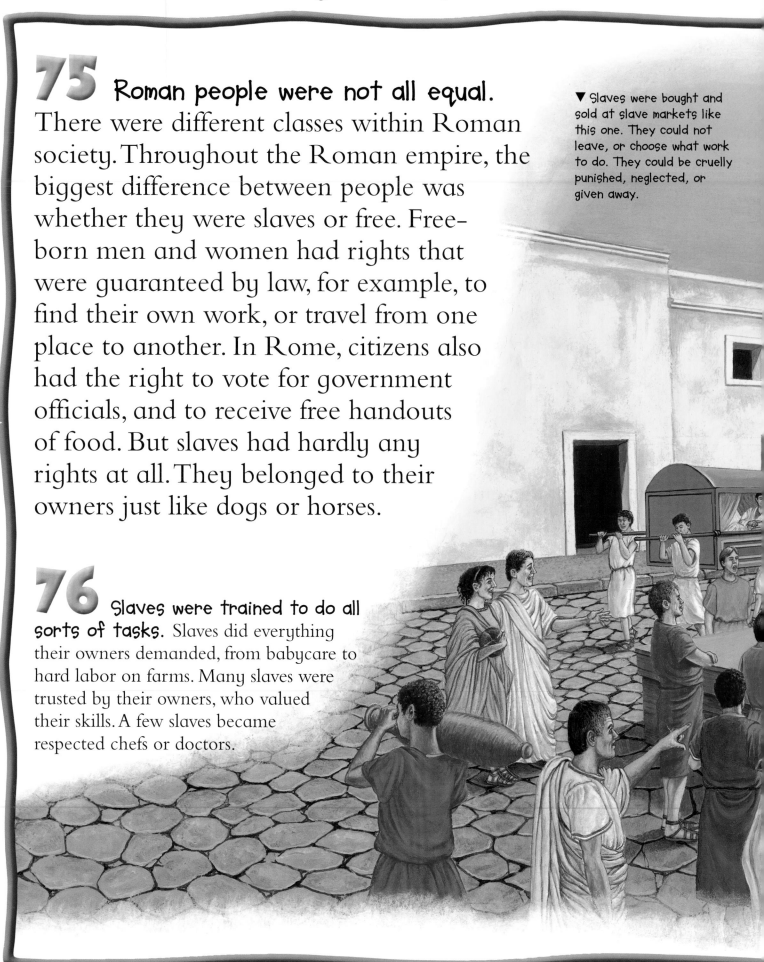

▼ Slaves were bought and sold at slave markets like this one. They could not leave, or choose what work to do. They could be cruelly punished, neglected, or given away.

76 Slaves were trained to do all sorts of tasks. Slaves did everything their owners demanded, from babycare to hard labor on farms. Many slaves were trusted by their owners, who valued their skills. A few slaves became respected chefs or doctors.

77 There were many different ways of becoming a slave. Slaves might be captured in war, purchased from a slave trader, or born to slave parents. They could also be people condemned to slavery as punishment for a serious crime.

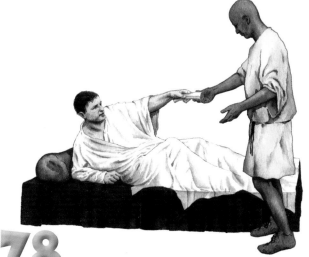

Slaves were paraded before the citizens to be chosen or rejected

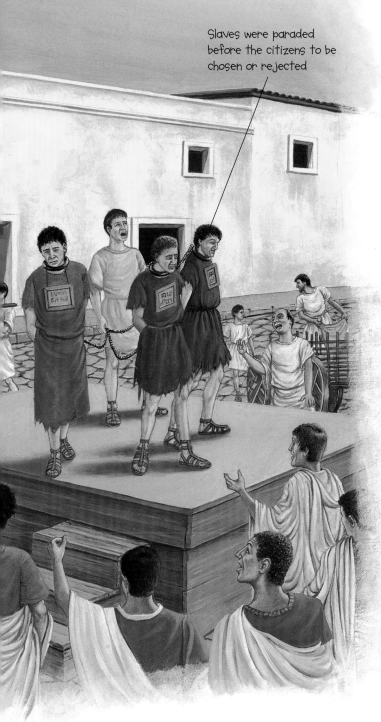

78 Slaves were sometimes set free by their owners. Freedom could be a reward for loyalty or long service. Some sick or dying slave-owners gave orders that their slaves should be freed. They did not want their slaves to pass to a new owner who might treat them badly.

I DON'T BELIEVE IT!

From 73BC to 71BC a slave named Spartacus led a revolt in southern Italy. He ran away to a hideout in the hills where 90,000 other slaves joined him.

79 Some slaves did very well after they were freed. Former slaves used the skills they had learned to set up businesses of their own. Many were successful, and a few became very rich.

Roman knowhow

80 The Romans pioneered many new building materials and designs. They discovered concrete, which was much cheaper and easier to use than solid building stone. They made bricks of clay baked at high temperatures which lasted much longer than unbaked ones. They found out how to use arches to create tall, strong walls and doorways. They designed massive domes for buildings that were too big to be roofed with wooden beams.

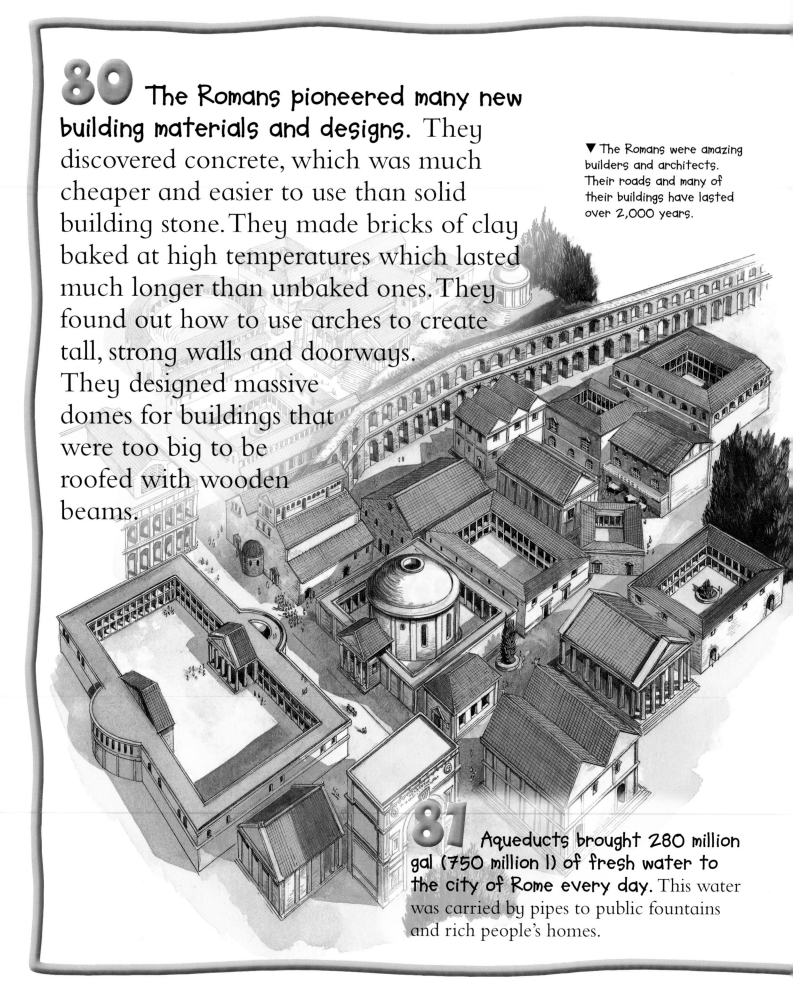

▼ The Romans were amazing builders and architects. Their roads and many of their buildings have lasted over 2,000 years.

81 Aqueducts brought 280 million gal (750 million l) of fresh water to the city of Rome every day. This water was carried by pipes to public fountains and rich people's homes.

▲ This is a Roman valve that allowed water to be pumped uphill. Water would then come out of fountains such as the one shown here.

I DON'T BELIEVE IT!

Our word "plumber" comes from "plumbum," the Latin word for the lead used by Romans to make water pipes. The same word is also used for a "plumb line," still in use today.

82 The Roman's water supplies were so advanced that no one had anything better until the 1800s! They invented pumps with valves to pump water uphill. This went into high tanks above fountains. Gravity pulled the water out of the fountain's spout.

84 Even the best doctors often failed to cure their patients. But Roman doctors were skilled at sewing up cuts and joining broken bones. They also used herbs for medicines and painkillers.

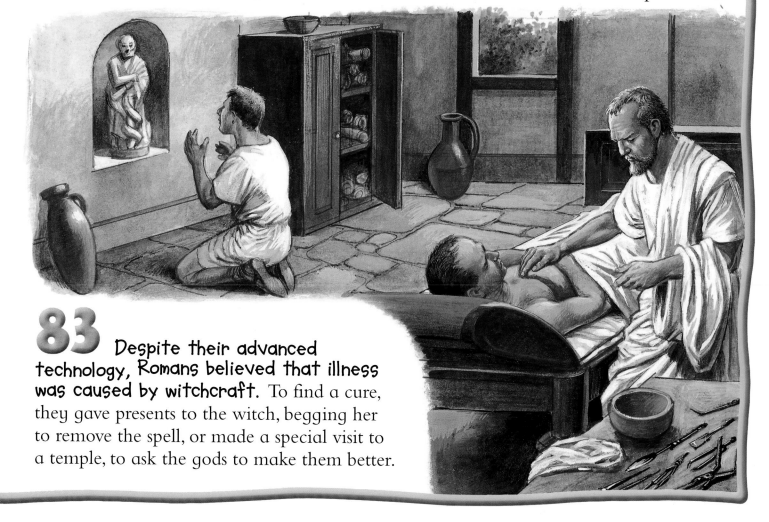

83 Despite their advanced technology, Romans believed that illness was caused by witchcraft. To find a cure, they gave presents to the witch, begging her to remove the spell, or made a special visit to a temple, to ask the gods to make them better.

Prayers and sacrifices

85 The Romans worshiped many different gods. Jupiter, the king of the gods, protected Roman lands. His wife Juno was worshiped by married women. Mars was the god of war, Venus was the goddess of love. Diana, the moon goddess, guarded young girls and wild animals. Neptune, god of the sea, sent earthquakes and terrible storms. Vesta was the goddess of Roman homes. Her priestesses tended a holy flame in a temple in the Forum in Rome.

Jupiter, king of the gods

Juno, queen of the gods

Mercury, messenger of the gods

Neptune, god of the sea

Mars

Venus, goddess of love

Minerva, goddess of war

Diana, goddess of the moon and hunting

Pan, god of the mountainside, pastures, sheep, and goats

Dis (Pluto), god of the underworld

86 The Roman emperor was also chief priest. As part of his government duties he said prayers and offered sacrifices to the gods who protected Rome. He was given a special name "pontifex maximus," which meant chief bridge-builder, because people believed he acted as a bridge between the gods and ordinary people.

87

Families made offerings to the gods every day. They left food, wine, and incense in front of a shrine in their house. A shrine is like a mini church. It contained statues of ancient gods called the "lares" and "penates." The lares were ancestor spirits, who looked after living family members. The penates guarded the family's food.

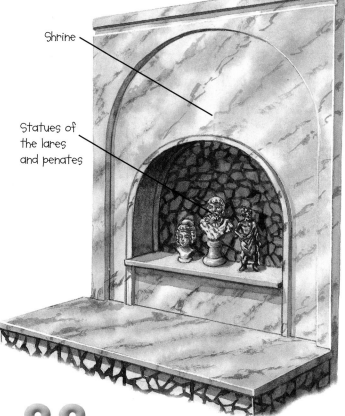

Shrine

Statues of the lares and penates

88

Roman people were very superstitious. They decorated their homes with magic symbols and hung good luck charms around children's necks. They believed that they could foretell the future by observing animals, birds, insects, and even the weather! For example, bees were a sign of riches and happiness but a hooting owl foretold danger.

89

Roman men and women could ask the gods to curse their enemies. They wrote their enemies' names, plus curse words, on scraps of metal or pottery and left them at temples. They hoped that the gods would see these messages, and harm the people named in them.

90

Some of the world's first Christians lived in Rome. But until AD313 Christianity was banned in the Roman empire. Christians met secretly, in underground passages called catacombs, to say prayers and hold services. They also used the catacombs as a burial place.

I DON'T BELIEVE IT!

After an animal had been sacrificed to the gods, a priest, called a "haruspex," examined its liver. If it was diseased, bad luck was on the way!

On the move

91 All roads led to Rome. The city was at the hub of a network of roads that stretched over 53,000mi (85,000km). They linked outlying parts of the empire to the capital, so that Roman armies or government officials could travel quickly. To make travel as quick as possible, roads were built in straight lines, taking the shortest route.

▲ This map shows the Roman Empire in brown, and the roads that they built in black.

92 Rome's first main road was built in 312BC. Its name was the Via Appia ("via" is the Latin word for road), and it ran from the city of Rome to the port of Brundisium on the south-east coast of Italy. Many travelers from Greece arrived there, and the new road made their journey to Rome quicker and easier.

93 Some Roman roads have survived for over 2,000 years! Each road was made of layers of earth and stones on top of a firm, flat foundation. It was surfaced with stone slabs or gravel. The center had a camber, a curved surface, so that rainwater drained away into ditches on either side.

Large surface slabs

Drainage ditch

Route accurately marked out

Solid foundations

94 Roman engineers used tools to help them make accurate surveys. They made careful plans and took measurements before starting any big building project, such as a new road or city walls.

▲ These road builders are using a "groma" to measure straight lines.

I DON'T BELIEVE IT!
The Romans often consulted a fortune teller or a priest before setting out on a long journey.

95 Poor people had to walk everywhere. They could not afford to hire a horse or a donkey, or a cushioned carriage, pulled by oxen. If they were lucky, they might manage to hitch a lift in a lumbering farm wagon—but this would not give them a comfortable ride!

96 Town streets were crowded and very dirty. Rich people traveled in curtained beds called litters, carried shoulder-high by slaves. Ordinary people used stepping stones to avoid the mud and rubbish underfoot.

97 Heavy loads often traveled by water. There were no big trucks in Roman times! Ships powered by sails and by slaves rowing carried people and cargo across the sea and along rivers. But water transport was slow and could be dangerous. Roman ships were often attacked by pirates, and shipwrecks were common.

▲ The Romans' knowledge of shipbuilding, as in this trading ship, came from the Greeks. The Romans, though, were not really sailors, and they did not improve the designs.

Digging up Rome

98 Large amounts of evidence survives to tell us about Roman times. Archaeologists have discovered the remains of many Roman buildings throughout Roman empire lands, including palaces, forts, walls, aqueducts, temples, hospitals, theaters, and ordinary family homes. They have also found Roman works of art, together with glittering gold and silver coins, beautiful jewelry, fine pottery, and delicate glass, and many tools and household objects used by Roman men and women in their daily lives.

Intricate Roman mosaic

These are lamps that burned olive oil for light

Statues can give us an idea what the Romans looked like.

99 We can still see many Roman designs today. Until the 20th century, grand, important buildings were often planned and decorated in Roman style. Architects believed that Roman designs inspired respect in anyone who saw them. For this reason, many big cities in Europe, North America, and elsewhere have churches, museums, art galleries, colleges, and even banks that look like Roman temples or Roman villas.

Roman pots

1. Who was the king of the Roman gods?
2. What is the proper name for a mini church in someone's house?
3. When was Rome's first road built?
4. What is the proper name for a curtained bed?

1. Jupiter 2. A shrine 3. 312BC 4. A litter

Roman people liked intricate and expensive jewelry

Roman coins show the most important people of the time, often the emperor

100 Many people still have Roman names. In many parts of the world, parents still like to give their children Roman names, or names based on Latin words. Here are some popular ones: Amanda (Loveable), Diana (Moon Goddess), Venus (Goddess of Love), Patricia (Noble), Laura (Laurel-tree), Virginia (Maiden), Julius (Roman family name), Antony (Roman family name), Martin (God of War), Marcus (God of War), Victor (Winner), Vincent (Conqueror).

▲ An archaeologist's dig uncovers remains from the Roman period. Their finds give us a better understanding of how the Romans lived.

Index